FIEL
DE TO THE NORTH AMERICAN BIRD

FIELD GUIDE TO THE

NORTH AMERICAN BIRD

Adam Blank with Lauren Blank

Illustrations by Michael H. Moore

TEN SPEED PRESS
Berkeley | Toronto

Ten Speed Press

P.O. Box 7123

Berkeley, California 94707

www.tenspeed.com

Distributed in Australia by Simon & Schuster Australia, in Canada by Ten Speed Press Canada, in New Zealand by Southern Publishers Group, in South Africa by Real Books, and in the United Kingdom and Europe by Airlift Book Company.

Cover and interior design by Headcase Design

Library of Congress Cataloging-in-Publication Data

Blank, Adam, 1970–

  Field guide to the North American bird / Adam Blank with Lauren Blank ; illustrations by Michael H. Moore.

     p. cm.

  ISBN 1-58008-574-1

  1. Obscene gestures—Humor. I. Blank, Lauren. II. Moore, Michael, 1970– III. Title.

PN6231.O26B58 2004

818'.602—dc22

2003024047

Printed in Canada

1 2 3 4 5 6 7 8 9 10 — 08 07 06 05 04

CONTENTS

ACKNOWLEDGMENTS

Without the initial support of Brett Martin, David Hirmes, and John Hodgman none of this would have happened. I want to thank all the nameless and faceless people who played the game with us and helped us enlarge our repertoire.

Thank you to my wife, Denise, for she not only handled a daily barrage of middle fingers while being pregnant with our first child, but she also acted as my creative mirror by giving them right back to me. To my new son Caleb, if I leave you with this book as my only legacy, then I have failed.

Finally, a young man who was of absolutely no help and actually attempted to deflate my confidence in the chances of getting this book published is Greg Emmanuel. If you ever run into this guy, please flip him the bird.

—Adam Blank

I'd like to thank both Adam and Mike for all the hard work and dedication they put forth to make this book happen. Without them there would be no bird book. Thanks to all the bird watchers out there who have watched and listened and shared their stories with us. This book is a compilation from many different people and places that all bond within the creativity of giving the bird. Lastly, thank you to that ubiquitous bird-giving spirit that exists within all of us.

—Lauren Blank

Many people throughout Iowa inspired the illustrations in this book, but especially my mother, my extended family, Lisa, Dimitar Krustev, Iowa's Strongest Man, Yuri, the entire Deal family, Floppy, Terry Branstad, and Chris Bruner.

And we must all thank the hardworking, industrious people at Ten Speed Press who saw the brilliance of our offerings when no one else would even return our phone calls.

—Michael H. Moore

THOSE WHO GAVE US THE BIRD

We would also like to acknowledge those trailblazing individuals who used their intelligence and creativity to discover new ways to flip the bird:

The Feather (page 28) was contributed by eight-year-old Lily Claar.

The Hair Flip (page 40) was contributed by Wendy Carriere.

The Cell Phone (page 44) was contributed by Paul Morris.

The Present (page 52) was contributed by Joshua Saul Beckman.

The Match (page 56) and **the Timber** (page 65) were contributed by Brett Martin.

The bong variation of **the Match** (page 57) was contributed by Kate Gerchenson.

The Chain Saw (page 74) was contributed by DJ Eurok.

The Kangaroo (page 92) was contributed by our older brother, Jared Blank.

The Windshield Wipers (page 93) was contributed by Matt Lawton.

The Heisman (page 94) was contributed by Oliver Jones.

Thanks for keeping the dream alive. You are an inspiration to us all.

PREFACE

Many years ago, in city far, far away called Des Moines, Iowa, siblings Adam and Lauren began flipping each other the bird. At first this gesture would elicit some reaction, usually resulting in one of them running to their mother to tell on the other. As time wore on, however, the bird became less and less effective. Eventually, they could sit for hours staring at each other with their birds exposed, stopping only out of boredom as their attempts to get a rise out of one another became more and more impotent.

Then one day all this changed when Lauren, who was sitting across from Adam with her right-hand bird fully upright, suddenly raised her left arm and extended a bird on that hand as well. Little sister trumped big brother. Her unprecedented move left Adam in a state of shell shock, or what today is better known as post-traumatic stress disorder.

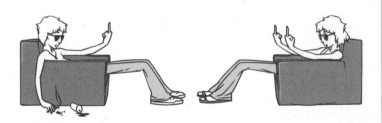

From that moment on, a combative form of bird display developed into what they called the Fuck-You Game. Lauren was always finding new ways to flip Adam off. At dinner she would grab the salt or pepper shaker with her middle finger extended. Or she would flip him off in a group setting by adjusting her glasses with her middle finger, and Adam would be the only one who knew what she was doing.

What began as sibling rivalry became a quest to answer the question, "Just how many ways are there to flip the bird?" After exhausting the classics, such as Peel the Banana (page 16), Read between the Lines (page 14), and the Scratch (page 20), they came up with ever more intricate and innovative techniques. Then they began to share the game with their friends, who, to their surprise, were eager to play along. Each time the game was shown to a new person, it would immediately break open the rusted floodgates of imagination and creativity normally constrained by the daily grind of the capitalist machine.

This book is a compilation of every birding technique they have come up with to date. It is an attempt to open a national dialogue on how best to give both loved ones and hated enemies the last bird on any subject. Some of these birds were created specifically for the game and might not be particularly effective in a hostile situation, but try them all. And remember that this is an interactive book: as you read, perform along with the pictures. See which styles fit you and which ones you just want to give . . . the bird.

INTRODUCTION

THE HISTORY OF THE BIRD

The bird is used by millions of Americans every day. It is given by the stars of the stage and screen to their directors, by administrative assistants to their bosses, and by junkies and bums to the middle-class people who walk by them on the streets and pretend they don't even exist. It is a gesture that is understood by rich and poor, black and white, young and old.

This gesture has been around a long time, but just how long? There are two major schools of thought on this subject. The first, and lesser known, contends that the bird reaches as far back as the Romans, who called the middle finger *digitus impudicus* or the "indecent digit." Advocates of this theory maintain the bird was used by emperors to insult their subjects, and they most often note that the emperor Caligula apparently used this deplorable gesture simply for shock value.

The second, and more popular, anecdote starts with the Hundred Years' War (1336–1565). Anticipating victory over the British, the French

decided to cut the middle fingers off of all their captured English soldiers, making it impossible for them to use the longbow so they would be incapable of fighting in future wars or uprisings. When the English won a major upset at the Battle of Agincourt (1415) they began mocking the French by waving their middle fingers at their defeated enemy, saying, "See, we can still pluck yew!" (The longbow was made from the wood of a yew tree.)

But those who help spread the rumor of the Battle of Agincourt are just as misguided as the Romanists. A recent revelation suggests the true origins of the bird might go back even further. The keepers of the true origins, the Heaven's Gate cult, were instructed to remain silent until the sixth coming of the Comet Hale-Bopp. The comet was supposed to signal the second coming of the Robot horde, calling the human race to prepare for battle. The cult members were instructed to disseminate their secret and ready themselves to be picked up by their alien ally, as their purpose on Earth had been fulfilled. When joyous moment came in 1996, they donned their space suits, Nike shoes, and khaki pants, and faxed their secret to every major English-speaking news agency on the planet. Then they drank a pitcher of "teleportation juice" (cyanide-laced Kool-Aid), and their essences were gathered by a passing spacecraft. On the opposite page you will find their largely ignored and widely dismissed press release, which reveals the true genesis of humanity and its most vile gesture.

In the year 7523 BC, Robots invented humans to gather raw materials for their war effort against their evil intergalactic enemies, the Blabacons. After humans had suffered a thousand torturous years as slaves, a young Neanderthal known as Bird Man (on account of his big nose) lead his people in a revolution. After three failed coups Bird Man discovered that if he placed his middle finger in a Robot's exhaust port, it would fill up with gas and pop like a balloon. He taught a small band of like-minded Neanderthals this tactic. They immediately mounted another revolt, and they were successful until they ran into some unexpected trouble with a group of their own people, whom they called the House Neanderthals. In a small skirmish with this highly trained, heavily funded unit, Bird Man was killed. Using his father's death as a battle cry, Bird Man's son took up the mantle of the revolution. With this gesture he led his fellow Neanderthals to victory over the Robot horde. We unknowingly honor our savior every time we flip . . . the bird.

So there you have it. From these humble beginnings evolved the North American Bird. And yew thought yew knew everything!

The manual is divided up into several families of birds that share common structural, situational, or thematic characteristics or that occupy the same habitat. Each series has an introduction describing the characteristics of the family—birds for work (page 39), birds for play (page 49), birds from around the world (page 83), and so on.

The birds themselves are broken down into four main parts: description, instructions, tips, and ratings. The description grants you access to the deep psychological underpinnings of the bird's origin, considers its sociological significance, or relates a historical anecdote. The instruction portion is self-explanatory. The tip is meant to help you develop more improvisation and spontaneity in your birding—so do exactly what we say.

And finally, the birds are rated on a scale of one to four in the terms of difficulty, impact, and specialty. One is the easiest and least offensive; five is generally more advanced, so proceed with caution if you're not a dexterous birder. Here's what the rating categories indicate:

Difficulty measures the level of skill one would need in order to actually perform the bird. For example, giving someone Read between the Lines (page 14) isn't going to tax anybody's dexterity and so would rate only one bird. The Fly Fisherman (page 64), on the other hand, requires timing, the use of both hands, a lot of improvisation, and panache, thus earning this gesture four birds.

Impact rates the bird's immediate visceral power. Try to imagine someone attempting to hurt your feelings with, say, the Saloon (page 95), which received a zero in this category. It wouldn't happen, and your response would most likely be one of confusion; you might even have to ask the birder for an explanation of this ineffectual bird.

Specialty gauges the bird's usefulness or applicability. You can pretty much walk around flipping the Vulgar (page 9) or the Pristine (page 8) to anyone for any reason and feel confident that your gesture is appropriate. However, some birds, such as the Trumpet (page 29) have more limited uses and require certain circumstances or habitats for effective execution. The more specialized the bird's use, the higher the rating.

Now that you have the tools to start birding, we hope you enjoy the book. And if you have invented or discovered a bird not covered in these pages, send it to us for review at submit@northamericanbird.com.

THE FINGERS OF THE HAND

When embarking on the difficult task of taming your wild North American Bird, it is important to start with learning the technical vocabulary. For that reason we have named the fingers of the hand in accordance with the popular American hand song. This little ditty was taught to you in preschool, and if you do not know the melody yourself, ask any friend of yours who actually passed the third grade.

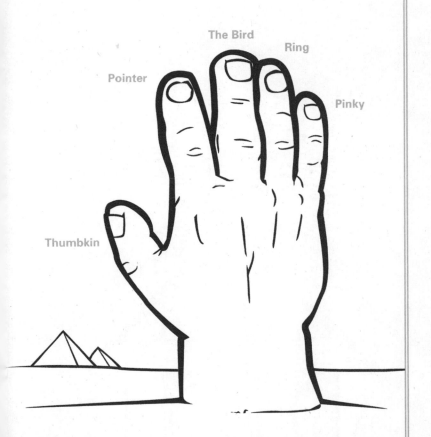

CHAPTER ONE

THE NEST

Through careful sociological observation and analysis, it has been determined that the North American Bird has two core, or "nesting," manifestations: the Pristine and the Vulgar. You must discover which of these makes its natural habitat in your hand.

You will be taken through both of these step-by-step. If you get lost before you get out of this section, you will have no hope of evolving to become a Master Birder. So be patient as these two are explained to those of you less-evolved individuals. You might need to refer back to the hand illustration (page 5) so that you can keep up with our terminology.

No matter which nesting bird you choose, we think that you will find either one particularly effective. And for those of you versatile enough to use both, kudos to you.

THE PRISTINE

Of course many people associate this gesture with a young Molly Ringwald flipping Judd Nelson the bird in *The Breakfast Club*. Though she later claims that she is not *that* pristine, her choice of bird says different.

INSTRUCTIONS

(1) Begin with the palm of your bird hand facing toward your body and your hand fully extended. **(2)** From the first knuckle, bend the pointer, ring, and pinky fingers down as far as they will go, in order to reveal the bird in its full glory. **(3)** Maintain a fully extended thumbkin for full prissy potential.

TIP Make sure your shirt collar is open wide enough to show off the brand new string of pearls Daddy bought you. This will express to the recipient, "My daddy loves me and will fire your daddy if I want him to."

DIFFICULTY: 🐦🐦 | IMPACT: 🐦🐦🐦 | SPECIALITY: 🐦

THE VULGAR

It has always been the position of the working class that if you are going to give the bird, it should have power. No points are given for style, just intensity and accuracy. To some the Pristine (opposite page) has neither of these two things, whereas the Vulgar executes both.

INSTRUCTIONS

(1) Begin with the palm of your bird hand facing toward your body with your hand fully extended. **(2)** Retract pinky, ring, and pointer fingers to the pad of your palm. **(3)** Swing thumbkin across the retracted fingers to hold in place. **(4)** Double-check that the bird is fully extended.

TIP A jaunty do-rag and soiled beater add a real sense of urgency to the Vulgar when paired with a missing body part or two. Give 'em hell, sailor!

DIFFICULTY: ⨉ | IMPACT: ⨉ ⨉ ⨉ ⨉ | SPECIALITY: ⨉

CHAPTER TWO

BIRDUS
CLASSICUS

Man has always disliked his fellow man for one reason or another (Look at that idiot's hair! Who does he think he is anyway? Do you *really* like that wagon wheel coffee table?). This is just human nature and an illustration of Darwinian social theory. You can't be better than someone else unless you can express how superior you are to them.

The basic birds in this chapter represent a gathering of the gestures that were created from the dawn of time until 1977, when Lauren was born and the true innovation began. You might see birds floating around the rest of the book that seem like they belong in this chapter, but keep in mind that we grew up in the Midwest, where the only fish we ate was at Red Lobster and the only classic birds we knew are in this section.

THE DOUBLE

This is most likely the first variation on the bird. Though its origins have been shrouded in mystery for centuries, we have unearthed them for you. Ten years after the Hundred Years' War, a small French child named Pierre was being taunted by a group of English kids. He flipped them the bird with his left hand, but then he remembered what his father had told him time and time again just before he received a thorough beating, "Being left-handed is a sign of the Devil." He immediately threw up a right-handed bird to correct his delivery, but forgot to disengage his left. The English children were shocked by what they had seen and ran home crying all the way. After being questioned by their parents about what had happened, they told the story of receiving the double insult of two birds at the same time. The parents were frightened by what they heard and formed a mob to subdue the child. He was later burned at the stake for being a witch.

INSTRUCTIONS

(1) Make a bird with one hand. **(2)** Make a bird with the other hand. **(3)** Display the birds to the recipient of your ire.

TIP For full effect timing is of the essence. After the first bird has been extended, wait until the recipient is about to deliver his or her witty retort and then spank them with the second. Taking it out from behind your back and making a crushing sound effect will also aid in its potency.

DIFFICULTY: 🦃　　　IMPACT: 🦃 🦃 🦃 🦃　　　SPECIALITY: 🦃

THE VOLUME

This bird has always been something of a butt-rocker move. But, if you are the type of person who used to cut class in high school to go out into the parking lot to listen to Led Zeppelin and smoke cigarettes without realizing that you would have years to sit on your ass at the gas station and smoke, then the Volume is truly for you.

INSTRUCTIONS

(1) Start this move with the bird pointing down toward your feet. **(2)** Grab your recipient's attention by asking, with a glib look on your face, "Can you hear this?" As this question really makes no sense, there is a good chance that they will simply stare at you. **(3)** That should give you just enough time to let loose with, "Do you want me to turn it up?" **(4)** as you simultaneously rotate your bird to an upright position. Then just sit back and watch the Volume blow them away.

Fig. A

Fig. B

TIP Even though this is a classic, you should practice several times with a friend before you take it out into public. Correct facial expressions and good timing will produce maximum impact. We suggest using the face Ozzy made after biting a bat's head off. Drool blood if you dare!

DIFFICULTY: 🦅🦅   IMPACT: 🦅🦅🦅   SPECIALITY: 🦅   13

READ BETWEEN THE LINES

You probably acquired this concept in your first good English or journalism class when you were taught that a turn of phrase could say one thing but mean something entirely different. Your teacher most likely drilled this concept into your head after you incorrectly scrutinized a quote that you were supposed to read between the lines. At this moment of your utter humiliation, the class smart-ass in the back of the room quickly retorted under his breath, "Read between these lines," at which point he became the hero of the class and the head cheerleader fell instantly in love with his quick wit. And all this happened while you just sat there and wished you could have been that guy.

INSTRUCTIONS

(1) Take your pointer, bird, and ring fingers with your palm facing you and hold them up in front of the recipient's face. **(2)** State clearly that they should, "Read between the lines." **(3)** Sit back and wait for them to get it. **(4)** Pat yourself on the back for being as witty as they come.

TIP Though this standard can be used for just about any occasion, it is best used on a younger crowd and is most effective right after you smoke your first bowl.

DIFFICULTY: 🦅 | IMPACT: 🦅 🦅 🦅 | SPECIALITY: 🦅

SIT (ON IT) AND SPIN

The origin of this classic dates back well before the mid-1970s, but its current manifestation has to thank the television show *Happy Days*. Ralph Mouth and his gaggle of friends used a G-rated version of this bird by telling the well-deserved receiver to simply sit on it. As time passed, because of its popularity and overuse, it was not insulting enough to just sit on it. In order to reemphasize its intended insult the receiver was also asked to spin on it.

INSTRUCTIONS

(1) Extend your nesting bird in the direction of the beneficiary of your ire. **(2)** As you say the words, "Sit on it," **(3)** slowly rotate your finger in a counterclockwise motion.

Sit on it, Potsie.

TIP You must truly believe that the bird's recipient is going to sit on it, and this is their punishment for being them.

DIFFICULTY: IMPACT: SPECIALITY:

PEEL THE BANANA

This gesture was the by-product of a little-known Nazi experiment. Knowing that all of Shakespeare's plays were written by a bunch of monkeys on typewriters, the Nazis created a similar setup believing their superior German monkeys would stumble upon an inconceivable weapon that would defeat the Allies. Using the Skinnerian model of operant conditioning, the Nazis enticed their monkeys' small successes with bananas, hoping it would eventually lead them to a scientific discovery of diabolical genius.

But the program did not produce results as quickly as Hitler had hoped. He placed intense pressure on the program manager, Sergeant Charles Schultz (later immortalized by John Banner on television's *Hogan's Heroes*), and Schultz began demanding more from his monkeys while doling out fewer treats. The monkeys organized a strike to get their well-earned rations back. Charles responded by peeling *this* banana, and in a minor victory for the Allies, the famished and rightfully pissed-off simians overthrew their Nazi captors and gorged on the sergeant's brains—*quite* the delicacy.

INSTRUCTIONS

(1) Raise pointer, bird, and ring fingers with your palm facing you. **(2)** Say, "Peel the Banana." **(3)** Drop your ring and pointer finger. **(4)** Stare at the recipient with intense and fanatical eyes.

Fig. A

Fig. B

TIP Use your other hand to carefully peel away the pointer and the ring finger. This slows down the process and makes the entire action even sleazier.

DIFFICULTY: | IMPACT: | SPECIALITY:

ADJUSTING THE GLASSES

Obviously this bird cannot work for everybody, but Adjusting the Glasses is where the pocket-protector, thick-tortoise-shell-frame, wearing-the-shoes-on-the-wrong-feet geeks really have a leg up on the rest of us. It's rumored that Bill Gates invented this one when a San Dimas High School football player was making fun of his accomplishments in the audio/visual club. Bill, recognizing that he could never match himself physically with this menace, decided to attack with a clever adjustment of the glasses. Bill felt quite pleased with his actions but realized that nobody else noticed his feat of brain over brawn. Later that day in physics class, where he normally gave Dr. Kirkpatrick his full and undivided attention, he daydreamed of a world where geeks could congregate and communicate with each other over vast distances from their own homes and talk of such achievements.

INSTRUCTIONS

(1) If you do not already own a pair of glasses—prescription, sun, or otherwise—obtain a pair. **(2)** Take said glasses and place each arm of the pair gently over the prescribed ear with the lenses and bridge sitting anywhere from slightly lower than the bridge of your nose to its tip. **(3)** Extend your nesting bird and place it on the bridge of your glasses. **(4)** Slowly push them up so they snugly fit upon your face. **(5)** Return your bird to its previous position.

TIP Let out a little sniffle when readjusting your specs. That is the way high school Bill would have wanted it.

DIFFICULTY: 🦃 | IMPACT: 🦃 🦃 🦃 | SPECIALITY: 🦃

THE REVERSAL

This bird could be the newest addition to the classics in over a 150 years. Like all great advancements in entertainment, art, and finger-gesture insults, the Reversal made its debut in Bollywood. After the partition of India, the great Mahatma Gandhi declared an end to Western cultural imperialism on the subcontinent. This left Indian superstar Nandamuri Taraka Rama Rao confused about how to handle a very emotional scene that was to take place on the next day of shooting. When the moment of truth came and his police officer character, Jayanth, was to raise his middle finger in the direction of the criminals who had stolen not only the money from the village but also his pride, he suddenly flipped his hand around and gave the villains the first-ever sighting of the Reversal. The director, B. A. Subba Rao, felt as though the metaphor worked for the film and left it in. This insult, with the help of such luminaries as Joyce DeWitt, Willie Aames, and Connie Chung, began to take root in America in the early 1980s.

INSTRUCTIONS

(1) Place your hand in the vicinity of the recipient's face with your palm facing them and your bird already fully extended. **(2)** Say in a loud voice, "Talk to the hand (you jive turkey)."

TIP When you use the Reversal you are not just giving your recipient the bird, but you are giving it to yourself as well. This can be helpful when showing that special someone your self-deprecating sense of humor—something that will help you end up in the sack every time.

THE SCRATCH

There is well-documented evidence that surfaced after the fall of the Berlin Wall that this bird originated in Tsarist Russia in 1092. The details are a little fuzzy, and the research team is still deciphering the ancient texts, but it looks as though one of the most ferocious games of cold shoulder was being played by a brother and sister, Ilya and Maria Ulyanov, twelve and eight years old respectively. After a day of taunting and teasing by her brother, Maria decided to give him the cold shoulder. She ignored him for days. No matter what Ilya tried, he could not get a response from her. At some point during this sibling showdown he began giving her the bird. She was astonished that he would go so far to infuriate her, so she ran to her mother to tell on him. By the time Ilya's mother confronted him about his alleged crime, he had withdrawn the offensive gesture and placed his bird upon his cheek and began to scratch. Being that both children were covered in pockmarks, the mother found no reason to punish Ilya.

INSTRUCTIONS

(1) Make your nesting bird, and **(2)** slyly place it somewhere on your body where only your recipient can see it. **(3)** Scratch away.

Fig. A

Fig. B

TIP Keep this as covert an operation as possible. If you are caught and the receiver confronts you, deny any wrongdoing and feign embarrassment over the whole ordeal, then as they turn their back on you to walk away, use your shillely.

DIFFICULTY: 🕊   IMPACT: 🕊 🕊   SPECIALITY: 🕊

CHAPTER THREE

BIRDS FOR
THE CHICKS

It wasn't until 1821 that kids were finally invented. It is almost impossible to imagine a world without them today. It is important to remember that they are not the tiny versions of adults that industrial England thought them to be. They have come a long way since the beginning and have secured new rights as wards of either their parents or the state. Some of the most important rights they have achieved as children are the right not to fall into large meat grinding vats and be served in assembly line cafeterias, the right to murder anyone they want and be released from prison at the age of eighteen, and the right to have their own portioned sizes at all reasonably priced eating establishments.

This section is just that, a child-size portion of the insult known as the bird. Of course, children's brains are not fully formed and kids have a propensity to like things that you can repeat over and over and over again, so please take this series of children-based birds with a grain of sugar.

THE BALLOON

The Balloon could definitely be placed in the classics section too because it is one of the earliest birds children get introduced to. We suggest you try this bird on any second-grader you can find. They will most likely blow you off with a nonchalant comment about how they learned that one last year and how behind the times you are.

INSTRUCTIONS

(1) Take thumbkin on your bird hand and bring it to your lips. **(2)** Blow into thumbkin as if you were attempting to blow up a balloon and simultaneously **(3)** extend your nesting bird. **(4)** With your alternate hand, pinch thumbkin at the base to hold the air in. **(5)** Pull the fully inflated bird away from your lips and display it to the recipient.

Fig. A

Fig. B

TIP Give yourself a couple of good breaths before the bird fully extends to add drama. To add a little variation to this classic, release thumbkin and let the balloon fly around and deflate. If you really want to give it to someone, you can let the deflating bird land on the recipient's face.

DIFFICULTY: 🕊️🕊️ | IMPACT: 🕊️🕊️🕊️ | SPECIALITY: 🕊️🕊️

THE HELIUM BALLOON

The concept for this bird came to Chad as he was about sacrifice his first-born child on a mountaintop in an attempt to win wacky Roddy Kilgore and his Morning Mayhem Crew's big KGGO Wacky Ride giveaway. The contest was very simple: do the craziest thing you can think of while on a webcast and be the 301st caller, and you could win floor seats to the Des Moines Penguins' opening night hockey game. Just as he was about to bring his hatchet down upon his three-year-old's head, a clown suddenly sprang from the bushes and offered him one of his helium balloons. So Chad killed the clown instead and his kid sucked all the helium from the balloons and talked funny for hours. He didn't win the tickets, but to this day Chad believes that the clown was heaven-sent.

INSTRUCTIONS

(1) Insert a fake hose into your fist. **(2)** Turn the fake helium canister on. **(3)** Slowly let your bird extend as if it were filling up with helium. At full extension, **(4)** crimp the balloon so as not to release any helium, **(5)** turn the helium canister off, **(6)** disconnect the hose, and **(7)** bring the balloon opening to your mouth. **(8)** Take in a huge gulp of helium while **(9)** slowly deflating your bird. **(10)** Hold your breath for a split second, and then **(11)** in a helium-induced high voice say, "Fuck you."

Fig. A   Fig. B

Fig. C   Fig. D   Fuck you . . .

TIP Doing this to a clown will guarantee you a seat in heaven's supreme court.

DIFFICULTY: IMPACT: SPECIALITY: 25

THE JACK-IN-THE-BOX

Jack had lost his way up the bean stalk and ran into the old Sea Hag from Popeye lore about halfway up. After they shared some tea and swapped tales of adventure, the hag made a pass at Jack, which he not so kindly declined. This hurt the Sea Hag's feelings, so she cursed Jack in almost the same way she cursed an Arabian gentleman about two thousand years earlier. He was to be forever locked in a small child's box, and his only hope for release would be if someone performed the proper song while twisting a little crank on the box's side. Once released Jack would have the option of sleeping with the Hag or returning to his cell. Needless to say we still have Jack in the box, and boy is he pissed.

INSTRUCTIONS

(1) From your elbow, extend your bird-giving arm out in front of you and **(2)** make a fist with your palm facing up. **(3)** Take your other hand and grab onto an imaginary crank handle attached to your fist. **(4)** Begin rotating the handle clockwise. **(5)** As you crank, hum the song "Pop Goes the Weasel." When you get to the part when you actually say, "Pop goes the weasel," **(6)** make a popping sound with your lips and **(7)** thrust your arm up while **(8)** extending the bird. **(9)** Let your bird hand bounce around a little as if it were on the end of a spring.

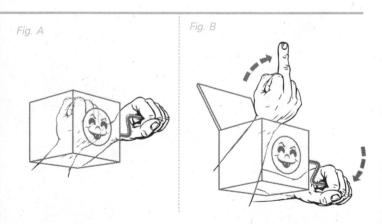

Fig. A

Fig. B

TIP This bird will make your children cry, so threaten them with it instead of a time-out.

DIFFICULTY: 🐦🐦🐦   IMPACT: 🐦🐦🐦   SPECIALITY: 🐦🐦🐦

THE TRANSFORMER

When using this bird it is important to really think of yourself as a robot, and not any lame robot like Twiggy or the Professor. The cooler the robot you pretend to be, the more effective the bird. Our top five robots are, in no particular order: the Robot from *Lost in Space*; Rosie from the *Jetsons*; Bishop from *Aliens*; Agamemnon from the *Odyssey*; and Dagget, the robot dog from *Battlestar Galactica*.

INSTRUCTIONS

(1) Begin by pointing at the recipient. **(2)** Make the sounds that transformers make when changing from a battleship to a robot or vice versa. **(3)** For each sound you make, change one position of your hand as if you were a robot. By our count there are only four sounds so make them all count. **(4)** As you make the last sound, make sure that you your best bird is standing.

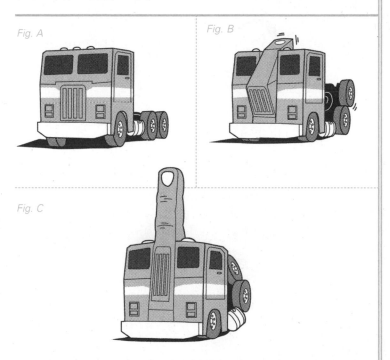

Fig. A

Fig. B

Fig. C

TIP Talk in a robot voice for at least three minutes after you use this bird. Then you will be really cool.

THE FEATHER

The old riddle goes, "Which is heavier, a pound of gold or a pound of feathers?" If anyone ever asks you this telltale sign of stupidity, respond with this bird. It is guaranteed to offend, and that person will never approach you again asking, "If a plane leaves Toronto heading for New York and crashes on the border, where do they bury the survivors?"

INSTRUCTIONS

(1) Place your bird hand, fully erect with your palm facing you, between your face and the recipient's. Going from left to right, **(2)** tap on the tips of your fingers with your other hand and **(3)** say, "Feather, feather, rock, feather, feather, blow," with "rock" being your bird and "blow" being a request for your recipient to cooperate. When you finally get them to blow, **(4)** retract all your fingers except the bird.

Fig. A

Blow.

Fig. B

TIP You can name any objects you like as long as the bird finger is the heaviest. But be cautious; if you try this bird without its feathers you might just lay an egg.

DIFFICULTY: | **IMPACT:** | **SPECIALITY:**

THE TRUMPET

For those of you who are musically inclined, the Trumpet will benefit you in a number of difficult situations. If you are in a high school marching band and your tyrannical director is pushing you too far and throwing a tantrum, or if you are in a funked-up swing band and you are just about to be assaulted by a group of inebriated jocks who are making fun of your inability to ever get laid, then you might want to lock your lips on this instrument and make a bird call. It might get you expelled or beaten up, but it will also make you the envy of all your horn-toting amigos.

INSTRUCTIONS

(1) Show the recipient your profile as **(2)** you place thumbkin of one hand to your pursed lips and your other thumbkin to the heel of this hand. **(3)** Mime as though you are playing a trumpet by wildly moving your pointer, ring, and bird fingers as if you were pressing down on the keys of the trumpet. At the same time **(4)** make sounds as if you were part of the Orenette Coleman trio until you are ready to unleash the fury that is the Trumpet. When you are ready, **(5)** hold a single note for an extended period of time while **(6)** extending your bird on each hand to its full height and grandeur as your other fingers retreat in the direction of your palm. Repeat.

TIP A trumpet isn't the only instrument you can use, so don't feel hemmed in by this example or even constrained to the brass section. You can also perform this ditty on a flute or a saxophone, with the bow of a violin, or even while pounding out Mozart's fifteenth sonata on a piano. This versatile musical bird sings beautifully in a variety of musical genres.

DIFFICULTY: 🖕🖕🖕🖕 | IMPACT: 🖕🖕🖕 | SPECIALITY: 🖕🖕🖕🖕 | 29

CHAPTER FOUR

BIRD PLUMAGE

Everyone knows that being stuck at home watching your four kids while the fifth one is out front working on the Dodge Charger is a drag. This is especially true when your loved one is off with their lover, who happens to be your best friend and your sister. All the daydreaming of being one of those rich, uptight white people who has at least one servant per kid and can't remember their children's names isn't going to make a your life any better.

These birds, on the other hand, will certainly give you the upper hand in the ruffling-feathers category when you finally get the chance to get out on a hopping Saturday night and strut your stuff. You won't be worrying that you are going to be left penniless with all the kids when you know you can pull the Contact (page 32) out in the middle of the divorce proceedings and look good doing it.

THE CONTACT

When Ponce de León was a child he ran with a pretty trendy crowd. When he got a little bit older, he started having vision problems. He went to Queen Isabella of Spain and asked for her counsel. He knew that he needed to somehow correct his eyesight because his job as an explorer required keen vision, but he knew that if his friends in the royal court caught him wearing spectacles he would have to face endless ridicule. The queen offered him a solution. She told him about a new invention called "contacts." Ponce was ecstatic. All his problems were solved until the fateful night of the big cotillion when one of them popped out of his eye. The entire room stopped dancing and watched as he bent down to retrieve the lens and place it back in his eye. Knowing that his social standing was lost until he could overcome his grotesque deformity of bad eyesight, he used his bird and gave everyone an eyeful before he marched out of the hall, never to be seen again.

INSTRUCTIONS

(1) Make an exclamation such as, "Oh my goodness gracious, I do believe I have just lost one of my contact lenses!" **(2)** Crouch down to the ground and behave as if you were searching for your missing optic. **(3)** Make a second comment along the lines of, "Ahhh, there it is." **(4)** Return to your previous standing position, but **(5)** have your bird extended as if you were balancing a contact lens on its tip. **(6)** Slowly raise your bird to your eye as if you were going to reinsert the lens.

TIP Pull your eye open with your other bird as you reset your fallen lens and think to yourself, "The double whammy . . . gotcha!"

DIFFICULTY: 🐦🐦🐦   IMPACT: 🐦🐦🐦🐦   SPECIALITY: 🐦🐦🐦🐦

THE MASCARA

Certainly, you have witnessed with amazement people applying their mascara while driving their car or riding public transportation on pothole-covered streets. The magic and grace in the Mascara's application make this bird particularly well suited for sharing with siblings or loved ones. For all you boys out there, remember that mascara isn't just for the ladies any more.

INSTRUCTIONS

(1) Make a bird with one hand and a fist with the other. **(2)** Loosen your fist slightly to create a small hole. **(3)** Dip your bird into the hole and **(4)** make a couple of up-and-down motions. **(5)** Extract your bird from the hole and **(6)** bring the side of the bird up to your eyelashes. **(7)** Apply several coats. **(8)** Stare at your recipient with a smug expression on your face.

Fig. A

Fig. B

TIP To free yourself from the fear of poking yourself in the eye, actually poke yourself in the eye. This way you not only get to flip someone off, but you also get their sympathy as well.

DIFFICULTY: 🕊️   IMPACT: 🕊️ 🕊️   SPECIALITY: 🕊️

THE LIPSTICK

This bird is too good to elaborate on, so follow it to the letter. Whether or not to include the Compact as part of the Lipstick was a hotly debated issue. Purists maintain these are stand-alone birds while others argue that birds of a feather must flock together. We have decided to include the Compact here as a tip so you can judge for yourself if it has any place next to the perfection of the Lipstick.

INSTRUCTIONS

(1) From your elbow, extend your bird-giving arm out in front of you and **(2)** make a fist with your palm facing up. Take your other index finger and **(3)** stroke your bird knuckle, **(4)** partially extending your bird with each stroke When it is fully extended, **(5)** run the tip of your bird across your top and bottom lips. **(6)** Purse and/or blot your lips. Retract your lipstick by **(7)** stroking your knuckle in the opposite direction while **(8)** gradually lowering your bird with each stroke.

Fig. A

Fig. B

TIP Once you've mastered the Lipstick, you might introduce it to its companion, the Compact: **(1)** After extending the Lipstick, **(2)** make a fist with your other hand and **(3)** place it in front of your face. **(4)** Using your lipstick bird, help your other bird out, as if you were opening a compact. **(5)** Place your compact bird in between you and the recipient and **(6)** stare into it as you apply your lipstick. **(7)** Close your compact and put it away.

DIFFICULTY: ✷ ✷ ✷   IMPACT: ✷ ✷ ✷ ✷   SPECIALITY: ✷ ✷ ✷

THE HAIR BLADE

The chances are pretty good that if you were ever a little boy, then you really wanted a switchblade but your overprotective parents refused, claiming that you would probably poke your eye out with one. You probably also remember the day you came home with your novelty switchblade comb. You took it out and showed your mother what looked like a blade. The moment before you got in trouble you pressed the blade-releasing button and out popped a short, narrow-toothed comb, which you ever so suavely dragged across your hair.

INSTRUCTIONS

(1) Make a fist. **(2)** Flick your fist from the wrist, while **(3)** extending your bird at the back end of the flip. **(4)** Place an optional pause here for maximum effect. **(5)** Then you bring your bird up to your hairline and drag it slowly across your hair while making a smarmy facial expression.

Where's your hairnet!

TIP Apply a smear of grease to your head and walk around like you are one of the lords of Flatbush. This might not increase the impact of your bird, but it will make you a little smarmier.

DIFFICULTY: 🐦🐦🐦 | IMPACT: 🐦🐦🐦🐦 | SPECIALITY: 🐦🐦

THE SNEEZE

This is the bastard child of the coughing insult. You might remember this witty move from your high school days in the early 1980s, when the substitute teacher would walk into the room and that one dude who thought he was the James Dean of your class, without ever knowing who James Dean was, would invariably cough and say, "Loser," at the same time. He would then proceed to daydream about how all the women would think he was such a rebel and how after class they would corner him in the hall, tear off all his clothes, and attempt to have sex with him right there in the hallway. He still has the same daydream today, as he stands around taking orders at the local Taco John's.

INSTRUCTIONS

(1) Bring your hand up to your face as if you were about to sneeze, in an attempt to lessen the saliva spray. **(2)** As you make a sound akin to a real sneeze, **(3)** extend your bird.

Fig. A

Fig. B

TIP You might try this bird with the coughing sound, but if you did you would be a *[cough]* LOSER!

DIFFICULTY: 　　IMPACT: 🦃🦃🦃　　SPECIALITY: 🦃

CHAPTER FIVE

OFFICE BIRDS

In America you were brought up to believe that hard work in school would get you into a good college, and being accepted to the right college would make all the difference in what job you would be able to get, and that would be the measure of your success. But instead what most people found out was that there are only a few people who actually attain the type of success promised by this urban myth. The rest of us worked really hard to attain the heights of mediocrity. We did what we were told, but we still all have people more powerful than us in the workplace, and we wonder how they achieved their heights considering that they are such idiots.

This collection of birds bestows upon ineffectual blue- and white-collar workers the precise tools necessary to express how they truly feel to those coworkers who would rat them out or steal their ideas in order to get a leg up. Remember the old adage: Those who are able to handle difficult situations with greater ease, grace, and style than their boss . . . will be able to get the last bird in.

THE HAIR FLIP

When trying to escape from some moron in management, the gals in office 101 pull this one out as an urgent signal to others in the know that they need someone to intervene. They are happy to share this effective technique with you, but they warn that you must never let the potential recipient figure out what you are really doing. If the information ever fell into the wrong hands, it would render this bird useless and leave you vulnerable to possible counterattack by management.

INSTRUCTIONS

(1) While listening intently to the recipient, **(2)** slyly extend your bird as you **(3)** bring it up ear level. **(4)** Use it to grab a lock of dangling hair that might be causing you problems at that moment. **(5)** Then use it to flip your hair back behind your ear. **(6)** Return your hand to its resting position.

Fig. A

Fig. B

TIP Make sure your hair is long enough to actually need flipping. Running your middle finger behind your ear with short hair is not recommended.

DIFFICULTY: 🐦🐦 | IMPACT: 🐦🐦 | SPECIALITY: 🐦🐦🐦

THE POINTER

In 1624 the first great meeting of the WASP collective gathered in Vienna to discuss a variety of issues concerning their status in the world. Item number 246 on the agenda stated: "Find a clandestine and completely deniable way to insult someone while maintaining an appearance of indifference." They formed a committee that worked tirelessly at the task at hand. The best that they could come up with was an action in which they pretended not hear what another person was saying. They called this the "cold shoulder approach." When the committee brought the report back to the convention the next year for discussion, a chairman who hated the proposal continually expressed his disapproval by pointing to it with his middle finger. The debate still rages on over which is the more effective way to surreptitiously insult someone.

INSTRUCTIONS

(1) Extend your bird and use it to point out items of interest to your recipient. **(2)** When you have finished pointing, retract your bird as if nothing had happened.

1. chlamydia
2. syphilis
3. herpes
4. salted nut roll

TIP If you are ever caught doing this, apologize for the miscommunication and say something like, "Oh, I am sorry, but in Iowa that is the way we point. I had no idea it would be considered offensive."

DIFFICULTY: ⤜ | IMPACT: ⤜ ⤜ | SPECIALITY: ⤜ ⤜ | 41

THE GRAB

Guitarists seem to do this to audiences all the time and no one ever says anything about it. They either put a slide on their bird or use it to clamp down across the fret board. But how are those of us who don't play the guitar supposed to use the Grab—especially those of us who need to use it on the sly in a work environment? The answer is simple: slide your bird through the handle of your coffee cup as you grab it to take a sip. You could transform yourself into Dr. Johnny Fever from *WKRP in Cincinnati* or Dave from *Talk Radio* and always have a coffee cup on you. Punctuate every remark by gesturing with your cup and your extended bird; nobody will think twice about it. Every time you make a toast to your boss at another self-aggrandizing event you can really be flipping him off. You could potentially be flipping everybody off all day all the time . . . sounds a little like heaven, doesn't it?

INSTRUCTIONS

(1) Find something to pick up with your bird. **(2)** Pick it up with your bird. **(3)** Hold it for a while. **(4)** Put the object back down (optional).

TIP If you work in service, you're bound to run into one jerk-off per hour who thinks you don't deserve to be treated like a human being. Your best recourse is to use the Grab to hand off the bill or receipt—after they've tipped, of course.

DIFFICULTY: 🐦 | IMPACT: 🐦 | SPECIALITY: 🐦

THE THINKER

The secret of Rodin's *The Thinker* is that originally his work was called *The Finger*. Two hundred years after its unveiling, Napoleon's troops invaded France and defaced all great public works of art by using them for target practice, making their way through all the great sculptures of the period. When they reached *The Finger* a cavalier young lieutenant, Marcus Cactus, took aim and casually shot off the protruding middle digit. Little did Napoleon's troops know that this act was to signal the counterrevolution, led by the young Mao Tse-tung, to begin an attack that would drive the invaders out of France and back into the sea. The statue has remained this way ever since and was renamed to capture the new feelings it evoked.

INSTRUCTIONS

In one fluid motion, **(1)** place your elbow on your knee or desk, **(2)** place your fist under your chin, **(3)** and extend your bird and position it on or about your forehead. **(4)** Think.

TIP At your next meeting, after your boss asks another stupid question about how the company operates, place the bird on your temple and furrow your brow as if deep in thought. Or, simply tap your bird on the table, thereby covertly flipping off your recipients and annoying them with your lack of rhythm while they wait for you to ponder their question.

DIFFICULTY: 🐦 | IMPACT: 🐦 🐦 🐦 | SPECIALITY: 🐦 🐦

THE CELL PHONE

C. W. Jensen was afraid of new technology. It took him several years before he bought his first computer even though all his peers had been using them for quite some time. When cell phones became common-place, his office mates tried to pressure him to move into the modern age by getting one for himself. One day when he was receiving a con-sistent barrage of jests at his expense, he told his friends to hold on for a second. He then reached into his pocket and withdrew his version of a cell phone for them all to enjoy.

INSTRUCTIONS

(1) Reach into your pocket or bag and pull your hand out with **(2)** your thumb and your bird fully extended. **(3)** Bring your hand to your head while **(4)** placing your thumb to your ear and your bird to your lips. **(5)** Answer your phone and then **(6)** pause as if your imaginary caller was asking for your friend. **(7)** Look surprised and say something like, "Sure she is, I'll get her for you right now." **(8)** Extend your arm and **(9)** rotate your hand to have the bird in an upright position as if to offer her the phone and **(10)** say, "It's for you."

Fig. A

Hello . . .

Fig. B

It's for you.

TIP Remember to keep the faux chitchat short or you can run the risk of ruining the punch line.

DIFFICULTY: 🐦 | IMPACT: 🐦🐦 | SPECIALITY: 🐦🐦

THE TYPEWRITER

When using *this* typewriter, it's worth it to verbally assault your recipient by dictating what you're typing. For instance, "Dear Mr. Dick Face: Thank you so much for your insensitive and insulting comments. I regard them in the same manner that I regard you. . . . " Continue in this manner as long as you need to—insult their mother and father, their attitudes toward farm animals, whatever seems appropriate. But don't get carried away; the Typewriter is a double hitter, so you should show your recipient a little mercy in what you dictate. You would not want to have to console the person you just put into hysterics.

INSTRUCTIONS

(1) From your elbow, extend your bird-giving arm out in front of you and **(2)** make a fist with your palm facing up. With your other hand **(3)** begin typing on the exposed portion of your bird-giving palm. With each key pressed **(4)** make a slight jerking motion to the left and **(5)** partially extend your bird. By the time you have moved your bird-giving hand as far left as you desire, your bird should be fully erect. At this moment take your typing fingers and **(6)** push your bird-giving hand back to the right as though you were manually returning the carriage. **(7)** As you slide your bird to the right it should retract to its starting position. **(8)** Repeat.

Fig. A

Fig. B

TIP Since most kids today don't even know what a typewriter is, you can choose to use the computer variation. Simply type out a short letter and say, "Print." Then make a funny printer sound as you raise your bird.

DIFFICULTY: 🐦🐦🐦🐦 | IMPACT: 🐦🐦🐦🐦 | SPECIALITY: 🐦🐦🐦

THE SALUTE

Considered out of fashion in military circles after the Bush presidency of the 1980s, this bird has migrated to the halls where most contemporary conflict occurs: the White House. After a long day of pushing paper to cover up your boss's support of the assassination of some minor dictator from a country that most Americans cannot pronounce, your boss comes in and places two new cover-ups on your desk. He insists that you finish them up before you leave for the day. You know that he will take full credit for the work that you do if it succeeds and will blame you if it fails. You have no choice but to complete the assignment because you need his endorsement when you run for the Sixteenth Congressional District next fall. Stuck between a rock and a hard place, you complete the shredding of sensitive documents that has to be done, but as you slide that one incriminating piece of paper into your trousers, you mumble a few expletives to your boss and give him the salute that he deserves.

INSTRUCTIONS

As the recipient is walking away **(1)** sit or stand in an erect military fashion. **(2)** Raise your arm as if you were going to salute them, but instead of extending all of your fingers, **(3)** extend just the bird. **(4)** Gently place it above the eyebrow of the same side as the arm you extended. Then, with a brisk snap from the elbow, **(5)** bring the bird down about six to eight inches.

Fig. A

Fig. B

TIP This bird can also be executed to enhance the recounting of a story about your boss or one of your coworkers to a group of friends over a beer. The only difference between what really happened and your new version is that now at the end of your story you actually do the Salute in front of your friends. You will all have a good laugh at how truly ineffectual you are as a person within the workplace because you were too afraid to do it at the time.

DIFFICULTY: | IMPACT: ——— | SPECIALITY:

CHAPTER SIX

PARTY BIRDS

There are those of you who like going out, getting drunk, picking someone up at a bar, taking them home, having lousy sex, waking up next to someone whose name you don't know, making up an excuse to get out of there, blaming your inability to find that perfect someone on other people, and puking. Others prefer getting off the job, meeting up with their dealer, snorting their purchase, going to a strip club, renting a prostitute, waking up early, and going back to work.

There are countless ways to party, and it all depends on your environment. But whether a Wall Street tycoon, a Kentucky redneck, a Virginian hillbilly, or a middle-class tire salesman with sensible shoes, people always feel the need to put on their crazy suit and get hepped up on their particular goofball. These birds are dedicated to those rugged individuals who aren't afraid of liver damage, lung cancer, STDs, or burning a hole in their heart from too much crank.

THE BOUQUET

During your first divorce you may feel some desire to confess all your sins and try to get back together with your ex-spouse. Nobody can argue with you that thirteen years of marriage is a hard thing to throw away, especially when kids are involved. But a truckload of roses won't make up for the fact that you were shtuping your neighbor, his wife, and their poodle trainer. For your second divorce you are little saltier. She was the woman you met in a hotel lounge in Detroit who you always knew was nothing but a gold digger, but you married her anyway because she had a great body and was twenty years younger than you. If you were divorcing her in the 1980s you might have sent a parting present of a dead fish or a bouquet of dead flowers in the mail. Today you get to give her this.

INSTRUCTIONS

(1) Fully extend all of your fingers and **(2)** wave them as if they were blades of grass being blown by a breeze. **(3)** Give your antagonist a steely stare and **(4)** ask, "What's this?" The recipient's response will most likely be a blank expression or something along the lines of "I don't know." **(5)** Quickly retract all your fingers except for the bird and **(6)** say, "It is a bouquet of these . . ." **(7)** Then, as you change from giving the bird to using your pointer finger to indicate just whom this bouquet is really for, **(8)** say, "just for you."

Fig. A

Fig. B

TIP Be careful with this bird: you might walk away with a pump or stiletto heel up your . . .

DIFFICULTY: 🦃🦃🦃🦃 | IMPACT: 🦃🦃🦃🦃 | SPECIALITY: 🦃🦃🦃🦃

THE PRESENT

This is the greatest Present story ever told, based on a true story of a man I will call Josh. For years, Josh and his sister played a game that matched their wits to find new and innovative ways to sucker each other into receiving the Present. The two were driving in tandem across the country from New York to California when Josh lost the game. In the middle of the night, in the middle of Nebraska, his sister began flashing her lights and honking. Worried, he pulled over to see what was wrong. She ran up to his car, hopped into the backseat, and said she desperately needed something she had left back there. After searching for a few minutes she let out, "Ahh, there it is." She came up from rummaging through the things on the floor and gave Josh her Present.

INSTRUCTIONS

(1) Reach into your pocket **(2)** as you say, "Hey, I got something for ya." **(3)** Pull your hand out of your pocket **(4)** with your bird fully extended, and **(5)** show it to your recipient.

Fig. A

Fig. B

TIP This is one of the most versatile birds around. For example, you can pretend to do a magic act and pull it out from behind someone's ear, your bra, or even your tight 1972 plaid bell-bottom pants. You can pull the Present out of just about anywhere, and the beauty of it is that its meaning is contained in its presentation.

DIFFICULTY: IMPACT: SPECIALITY:

THE CORKSCREW

If you ever find yourself surrounded by one those obnoxious wine-tasting crowds, use this handy bird to extricate yourself. When César Chavéz created the Corkscrew in 1972, he had been invited to discuss the plight of Mexican immigrant labor at a black-tie function hosted by some knee-jerk liberal foundation in San Francisco. He decided to attend, believing that he could drum up support from upper-class Bay Area white people. But on arrival, he realized immigrant labor was just their token minority cause of the week; they were more interested in talking about Napa Valley wines than about the exploited workers who picked the grapes. He responded by uncorking this bird for his hosts and then stormed out. The rest is history.

INSTRUCTIONS

(1) Make a fist with one hand and **(2)** a bird with the other. **(3)** Loosen your fist to create a small hole. **(4)** Screw your bird into the hole. Once it is securely fastened in the imaginary cork, **(5)** make some twisting motions and **(6)** extract your bird while **(7)** making a sharp popping sound. **(8)** Turn the bird right side up.

TIP This motion can be applied to anything you might be able to stick your finger into. Take that as you will.

| DIFFICULTY: 🦅🦅 | IMPACT: 🦅🦅🦅 | SPECIALITY: 🦅🦅🦅🦅

THE SOBRIETY TEST

We can all thank Nancy Reagan's Just Say No campaign for this bird. Though the War on Drugs has not decreased the number of people drugging and drinking, it has increased the number of people who make it their business to assess your state of intoxication. When such a person calls your sobriety into question, keep in mind that the drunker you are, the more difficult this bird is to pull off. If you happen to be sober, you have a number of great flourishes at your disposal. Our favorites are to miss your nose entirely, to poke yourself in the eye and then fishhook your mouth, or to accidentally slap the recipient in the face with both birds.

INSTRUCTIONS

(1) Extend both arms out as far as they can go. Simultaneously **(2)** close your eyes and **(3)** extend both of your birds. **(4)** Bending from your elbows, swing both birds toward your face and attempt to touch the tips of your birds to the tip of your nose.

TIP We don't recommend using this bird on a cop. We have noticed that it can have an adverse effect on the outcome of your interaction.

DIFFICULTY: 🖕🖕🖕   IMPACT: 🖕🖕🖕   SPECIALITY: 🖕🖕

THE MATCH

If you are a good mime, as most Midwesterners are, you can apply this action to numerous activities. The application that sticks out most prominently would be to mime the lighting of a cigarette. Then you are cool for smoking, flipping someone off, and blowing smoke out of your mouth all in good miming style. You will be the hat trick of hip.

INSTRUCTIONS

(1) Strike your fist across your other palm and **(2)** immediately extend your bird. If it doesn't work the first time, repeat the first step until it lights. **(3)** Hold it up to show the recipient. **(4)** Light your cigarette. **(5)** Blow on your bird and **(6)** retract.

Fig. A

Fig. B

TIP If you are really ready to party, use the Match to light a bong: **(1)** Place thumbkin's nail from your other hand on your lips **(2)** with your bird fully extended. **(3)** Bring the Match to your bong bird and suck in while making gurgley sounds. After you have taken a full hit, **(4)** hold your breath, **(5)** blow the Match out, and **(6)** in your best Jeff Spicoli–like surfer-dude voice say, "Fuck you . . . dude."

If a lighter is more your style, here's a variation for you: **(1)** Make a fist **(2)** with thumbkin sticking straight up into the air. **(3)** Strike it several times across your pointer finger. With the last strike **(4)** extend your bird, then go about your business of lighting a bong or cigarette. Do not use this variation if you are lighting a cigar; purists believe the butane does not mix well with a Connecticut shade wrapper.

THE JUNKIE

Let's say that your mother has set you up on a blind date . . . again. You decide to go because you want the old woman off your back and don't want to let on that being thirty-four in a midlevel job that is going nowhere and barely pays the rent is enough for you. You need backup in case you've been matched with a real dud, so you ask a couple of friends to show up at the date location. When you finally meet your date they talk incessantly about themselves, and you can't get a word in edgewise, even to excuse yourself so you can go ram your head against a wall. In such a situation, the Junkie is the bird for you. When your date's not looking, use it to signal to your friends to bail you out.

INSTRUCTIONS

(1) Extend your bird with (2) your palm fully open. (3) Place the tip of the bird in the crook of your other elbow. (4) Slowly collapse your palm as though its contents were being injected into your arm, while (5) slightly slumping over or making gagging sounds as if you were going to puke.

Fig. A

Fig. B

TIP While this bird can help you express to those around you that you are stuck interacting with a self-obsessed moron, it is a powerful weapon so be cunning about using it. Two individuals once gave the Junkie to each other at the same time and, needless to say, they blew up.

DIFFICULTY: 🦅   IMPACT: 🦅🦅🦅   SPECIALITY: 🦅🦅   59

CHAPTER SEVEN

BIRDS FOR THE OUTDOORSMAN

Growing up in Des Moines, Iowa, we all had a healthy respect for the long-standing traditions of hunting deer and pheasant; skinning a fresh kill and perhaps drinking its blood; torturing opossums and setting them on fire; and firing up the gas grill, sitting back after a long day on the killing floor, and tossing back a couple of tall cool ones. We also know that this upbringing taught us the meaning of the words "love," "friendship," and "community values" that perhaps some of you backstabbin', moneygrubbin', Italian suit–wearin' city slickers wouldn't understand.

The birds in this section are dedicated to our brethren back home who drink canned Schlitz and Hamm's out of the backs of their beat-up 1978 Ford pickup trucks. Some of these birds are sophisticated and might take more than one attempt to pull off, but they should bring out the dentally challenged mul-let lovers in all of us.

THE GARDENER

Sometimes the best comedy comes from getting someone deeply involved in a gag that ultimately has little payoff. The joke is on them, and the humor is for you. In the world of comedy, we call this the Andy Kaufman principle. Before you get your hands dirty with this bird, you should master this principle, as the end result is to make your recipient mad not because they received the bird but for having waited so patiently bird-watching.

INSTRUCTIONS

(1) Make a fist with your bird hand, palm facing up, and extend it out in front of you. **(2)** Mime the digging of a small hole and **(3)** the planting of a seed on top of your extended fist. **(4)** Water your fist with your invisible watering can. Each time you give your fist a little water, **(5)** your bird should grow just a little bit. After several waterings, **(6)** your bird should be fully extended.

Fig. A

Fig. B

TIP You really need to draw this one out. The longer the buildup, the greater the Kaufman principle.

DIFFICULTY: 🐦🐦🐦🐦 | IMPACT: 🐦🐦🐦 | SPECIALITY: 🐦🐦🐦🐦

THE STRONGMAN

Have you ever had sand kicked in your face at the beach? Your lunch money taken from you after you were given a toilet-bowl bath? Baklava smeared in your face by the imam's rebellious son? This bird, which is dedicated to Iowa's Strongest Man 1999, is the perfect response to all the bullies in your life. These people might be bigger and stronger than you, but as they are pummeling you to a pulp, just remember: they can't beat your wit out of you, only your desire to use it.

INSTRUCTIONS

(1) Fully extend your bird-giving arm out in front of you and **(2)** ball your hand up into a fist. **(3)** Make a fist with your other hand and, in a sweeping move, **(4)** bring it down onto the crook of your elbow. As you strike yourself, **(5)** jerk your extended forearm up to a vertical position, while **(6)** fully extending your bird.

Fig. A

Fig. B

TIP This is a feat of strength, so it might take a couple attempts to get your bird fully erect. When you finally get your bird all the way up, make a "ding" sound to get the attention of any casual observers so that they get an eyeful of your bird's proud plumage.

THE FLY FISHERMAN

Ben Franklin was an expert fisherman throughout most of his years. He used to take off from the Continental Congress every weekend with Grover Cleveland to visit a little fishing hole just outside of town. The trick was to always sidestep John Hancock, who was a bit of a loudmouth know-it-all whom neither of the two men could stand. Every now and then John would latch onto the duo's plans and ruin the entire outing. To get even, Ben and Grover used to incessantly make fun of their unwanted friend. Not the brightest guy in the world, John rarely caught on. On one such outing to the fishing hole when John was being particularly annoying, Ben announced that he had caught a fish, but when he reached down into the water, he came back up with this bird. Grover thought this was so funny that he had to tell Alexander Hamilton and Archie Carbunkle, who each told two friends, and so on, until the entire Congress was casting imaginary lines out and pulling up birds every time John came around. Guilt ridden for having hurt his feelings, they made it up to him by letting him sign the Declaration of Independence first.

INSTRUCTIONS

(1) Flick the wrist of your rod-and-reel hand toward your bird hand, while **(2)** extending your bird-giving arm as if you were going to catch the casted line. Instead of catching it **(3)** act as if you hooked your bird when the hook and your catching hand meet. **(4)** When you pull your rod back, simultaneously extend the bird of your caught hand. **(5)** When you relax your rod, retract your bird.

TIP Bring the Gun (page 70) so you can pop a cap in the fish's ass after you reel him in.

DIFFICULTY: 🐦🐦🐦🐦 | IMPACT: 🐦🐦🐦🐦 | SPECIALITY: 🐦🐦🐦🐦

THE TIMBER

When the protests over clear-cutting in spotted owl habitat started making national headlines and the five o'clock news, as usual the liberal press left out the most dynamic aspect of the story. While all the lumberjacks were waiting for the bondage-loving tree huggers to be unchained so the unbridled rape of our natural resources could continue, the lumberjacks were barraged with dim-witted hippie curses and chants, which were supposed to open the minds of the loggers to the beauty and importance of nature. A young lumberjack named Brett Martin, later described by his neighbors as a soft-spoken man, decided that there was no reason to engage in dialogue with the eco-revolutionaries, so instead he pulled the Timber out of his hat. He was soon arrested for indecent exposure and first-degree murder when a thirty-two-year-old hippie's heart immediately exploded upon witnessing the display.

INSTRUCTIONS

(1) Place your bird hand between you and the recipient with **(2)** all your fingers fully extended and your palm facing toward you. **(3)** Take the pointer finger of your other hand and run it back and forth across the knuckles of your elongated fingers. **(4)** Say, "Timberrr!" and **(5)** have all your fingers except your bird retract. **(6)** Feel good for saving a tree.

Fig. A

Fig. B

Timberrr!

TIP To really drive your point home, knock out one of your front teeth and don a tuque.

DIFFICULTY: 🕊🕊   IMPACT: 🕊🕊🕊   SPECIALITY: 🕊🕊🕊🕊

THE SKEET SHOOTER

This bird is a little tricky because it requires having at least one accomplice, but the payoff is worth it. The more people you can train to act as your skeet, the more impact the bird will have. For example, imagine that you are out with four of your friends and one makes an idiotic statement. You simply yell, "Pull," and six arms jut up into the air. You deftly aim and shoot, and your friend gets six birds at once. This action will send him running to the nearest fallout shelter in search of cover.

INSTRUCTIONS

(1) In advance, train your accomplices to hoist one fist after the other into the air at your cue. When you're ready to execute the bird, **(2)** yell, "Pull" and **(3)** take aim with your imaginary shotgun. When your accomplices' skeet hands are fully extended, **(4)** shoot your gun while making sounds that mimic bullets being fired. As you exclaim, "Pitchoo, pitchoo," your colleagues should **(5)** quickly transform their fists, one after the other, into birds and **(6)** let them drop from the sky for the recipient to see.

Fig. A

Fig. B

Pitchoo!

TIP This bird works best if you've actually fired a gun before, so all longhairs need not apply.

DIFFICULTY: 🐦🐦🐦🐦 | IMPACT: 🐦🐦🐦🐦 | SPECIALITY: 🐦🐦🐦🐦 | 67

CHAPTER EIGHT

BIRDS OF PREY

War is a terrible thing, whether it pits families against families or nations against nations, and devastation of any kind can sharpen one's awareness of their own mortality. Such recognition can create unstable individuals who are reckless, maybe even dangerous. If you fall into this category, you might have use for these lawless, aggressive birds. You just have to ask yourself, are you tough enough to give them a try? Well, are you . . . punk?!

THE GUN

Legend has it that Billy the Kid was surrounded at the Alamo with his trusted partners Davy Crockett and Pat Boone. After a three-day siege the entire Cuban army could not dislodge these men from their duties as American citizens. At the end of the first day they ran out of food, and Billy called for the men to hold their ground. At the end of the second day they ran out of water, but Billy still asked them to hold their ground. At the end of the third day they ran out of ammunition, but Billy devised a plan. At the count of six the three men jumped up and used the Gun against their adversaries. They were killed on the spot, and the Alamo fell, but several of the Cuban 101st light infantry division needed therapy for several years after the incident. Way to go, you American heroes.

INSTRUCTIONS

(1) Point your bird at your recipient. **(2)** Extend thumbkin so that he is pointing directly up in the air. **(3)** Make shooting noises that correlate with **(4)** slight kickback motions of your wrist as you fire your Gun.

TIP An alternate way to perform this bird is to create a gun with pointer and thumbkin, take aim at your other hand, and shoot off all the fingers, leaving only your bird standing.

DIFFICULTY: 🐦🐦 | IMPACT: 🐦🐦🐦🐦 | SPECIALITY: 🐦🐦

THE BOMB

Mr. Molotov was a slight man from a tiny town in northern Uzbekistan. He was as reclusive as the Unabomber and as sharp and cunning as the Shoe Bomber. His only problem was that he was unable to get the worldwide acclaim he felt was his due. He was honored that people were using his cocktail in myriad events, like revolutions, civil wars, and ethnic cleansings, but he regretted that they never made the connection between the bomb and his last name. He submitted this bird to us just days before a freak explosion in his lab. Ironically, he suffered such severe burns from the accident that he died from the injury.

INSTRUCTIONS

(1) Extend both arms forward so they are shoulder height and width apart. **(2)** Make a fist with each hand. **(3)** Your bird hand, the bomb hand, should have its palm facing up, and **(4)** your other hand, the plunger hand, should be palm facing down. **(5)** Push down slightly on the plunger, maybe eight to ten inches, to detonate the bomb. **(6)** Wait about three seconds, and then **(7)** raise your bird while **(8)** making a small explosion sound.

Fig. A

Fig. B

Boom.

TIP Instead of using a plunger to detonate the Bomb, use the Match (page 56) to light its fuse, thereby inflicting an irrefutable Double (page 12).

DIFFICULTY: 🦅🦅   IMPACT: 🦅🦅🦅   SPECIALITY: 🦅🦅

THE BOW AND ARROW

What do Douglas Fairbanks, Kevin Costner, and Patrick Bergin all have in common? They all played the bow-wielding Marxist superhero Robin Hood. Robin was most well-known for righting the wrongs of the rich, redistributing their wealth to the poor, and wearing tights. The only man who stood in his way was the Sheriff of Nottingham, defender of the rich. Like Robin, we each have our own Sheriff of Nottingham. Yours might be the young guy walking across the street against the light when you are in a hurry or the lady at the Chinese food restaurant who can't understand your accent when you place an order over the phone. Unfortunately, in contemporary America, if you are subject to such an injustice you can't just shoot your antagonist with an arrow. Today you must use your wits, so take aim with this bow and arrow and blow your Sheriff of Nottingham away.

INSTRUCTIONS

(1) Reach out with your non-bird hand and **(2)** grasp an imaginary bow. Using your bird **(3)** grab the imaginary bowstring and **(4)** pull it back to your cheek. When you **(5)** release the bowstring, **(6)** thrust your arm forward and **(7)** fully extend your bird.

Fig. A

Fig. B

TIP Bring your arrow right up to your recipient's face and proclaim, "Take that you evil Sheriff o' Nottingham–like individual." This should add that bit of spice that makes a good meal great.

DIFFICULTY: IMPACT: SPECIALITY:

THE SWITCHBLADE

Since the invention of guns and nuclear warheads, the knife has really taken a backseat in the category of most-feared weapon. However, during the height of the Cold War in the 1980s, two great actors, Sylvester Stallone and Paul Hogan, incessantly toiled to resurrect the knife as the weapon of choice—Sly with his giant blade with the serrated edge and the handle that concealed a sewing kit, and Paul with his crocodile-hunting saber. Though it was nationally agreed upon that the croc-killing blade wasn't nearly as cool as Sly's weapon, Mr. Dundee's quip, "That's not a knife, now *that's* a knife," became a mantra for the hip crowd. We are dedicating this bird to you fellas for the impact you had on people alive in the 1980s. Keep up the good work.

INSTRUCTIONS

(1) Make a fist with your bird hand. (2) Flick your fist from the wrist, while (3) extending your bird at the back end of the flip. (4) Add an optional pause here for maximum effect. (5) Then bring your bird up to menace your recipient.

Fig. A

Fig. B

TIP You can also use a variation that was very popular among the stoner ninjas at our high school, the Butterfly Knife. (1) Take your fist and move it around like a nunchaku while (2) you make the appropriate metallic sound effects. (3) End with your bird extended in front of your recipient. The stoner ninjas were usually the coolest kids in school, so you would be wise to imitate them.

DIFFICULTY: IMPACT: SPECIALITY:

THE CHAIN SAW

When Stuart Lebner was a child, the townspeople of Okeechobee, Texas, considered him a little odd. Stuey, as he was referred to, was infatuated with knives, axes, handsaws, and chain saws. At the age of six he could talk for hours about the master sword makers of ancient Japan or the pros and cons of the eight-inch, full-tang chef's blade versus the three-quarter tang. At the age of nine he convinced his parents to get in the family station wagon and drive to New London, Ontario, for the Scottish Highland games, where he first got to meet his hero Vince Ferragamo, five-time champion of the Hot Saw competition. His parents were a bit worried about Stuey's obsession, and their fears were justified on April 20, 1972, when during recess he was trying to have a conversation about cutting implements with a couple of classmates. One of the classmates, Pat Holtzman, son of a midlevel NASCAR racer, reacted to Stuey's enthusiasm by presenting him with the Chain Saw. Coincidentally, on that very same date, the Holtzman family reported the first appearance of Leatherface.

INSTRUCTIONS

(1) Give your recipient the bird. **(2)** Act as though you were grabbing a starter cord from the palm of your bird hand and **(3)** give it a yank. **(4)** As you yank make a noise that closely approximates the sound of a chain saw trying to start. **(5)** Repeat steps 3 and 4 until the chain saw fully fires and **(6)** make a continuous sound once it is on. **(7)** Vibrate your hand in accordance to the sounds you make.

Fig. A

Fig. B

TIP For anybody who has ever cut off their own hand and replaced it with a chain saw, this bird will feel like a natural extension of your body. Use that feeling.

DIFFICULTY: 🦅🦅🦅   IMPACT: 🦅🦅🦅   SPECIALITY: 🦅🦅   75

CHAPTER NINE

MECHANICAL
BIRDS

There are very few things that separate human beings from animals. For the most part our DNA is the same and we have the same needs like food and shelter. Something that does differentiate us, however, is our use of tools. We can thank Charles Surace, an Italian priest who, in a monastery in the Canadian Alps, invented the first group of tools, called simple machines: the lever, the inclined plane, the wheel, the axle, the screw, the wedge, and the pulley. This series of birds expresses the ingenuity of industrial man in his effort to mold the world in his image, in mass quantities. Like Henry Ford said, "Hitler is good, but machines are better."

THE CRANK

At the end of the nineteenth century, a German professor known as Sigmund Freud became infatuated with all things erect and joined a group called the Mechanists, who were dedicated to finding a scientific cure for all things not erect. Along with distinguished professors in Vienna, London, and Paris, he experimented with hypnotism, voodoo, prayer, and other controversial methods, but those techniques proved fruitless.

Finally, Freud enlisted the help of his friend Martin Buber, a great military engineer. At a famous Mechanist conference, they unveiled a promising contraption that, when cranked, would heighten things that were not previously heightened. When it failed to go up, the entire auditorium erupted in laughter, and Freud retaliated with the Crank. He was dismissed as a madman and ostracized from the scientific community, but today we know that we are all standing on the shoulders of giants.

INSTRUCTIONS

(1) Make a fist with your bird hand, your knuckles facing the recipient. **(2)** Take your other hand and grab an imaginary crank handle attached to your fist. **(3)** Begin rotating the handle clockwise, and in correlation to the turning of the handle, **(4)** raise your bird. **(5)** You are done when the bird is fully extended.

Fig. A

crankshaft

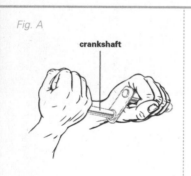

Fig. B

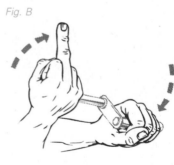

TIP Old Sigi gave new meaning to the saying "A bird in the hand is worth two in the bush."

78 | DIFFICULTY: | IMPACT: | SPECIALITY:

THE LEVER

Nobel prize–winning physicist Hal Stodimire won his award when he proved that the energy applied to a fulcrum is in direct proportion to the energy expended by the vectoral velocity of a falling body, or $E = V \times M/14.4$. Organic chemist Veronica Halbertum became enraged by the news of his impending award because he had stolen the formula from her. Hal, a misogynist, never truly believed that a woman could be smart enough to be a scientist, so he felt completely justified in taking credit for her work. At the ceremony in Oslo, Veronica protested outside with a picket sign that read, "The energy applied to this bird is multiplied by the strength of my malice $E \times M = $ 🖕."

INSTRUCTIONS

(1) Extend both arms a comfortable distance out in front of you with **(2)** your bird hand about shoulder level in a fist with **(3)** your knuckles facing the recipient and your palm facing up. **(4)** Place your other hand at eye level in a fist with your palm also facing up as if you're about to pull down on an imaginary lever. **(5)** Pull down on the imaginary lever while **(6)** simultaneously extending the bird on your other hand.

Fig. A

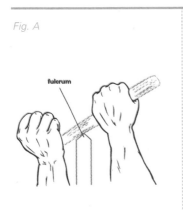

fulcrum

Fig. B

TIP Take Veronica's advice and use a bigger or smaller lever to work a heavier or lighter bird when you show your recipient exactly where to stick the fulcrum.

DIFFICULTY: 🖕🖕   IMPACT: 🖕🖕🖕   SPECIALITY: 🖕

THE PULLEY

A longtime favorite of the construction worker set, the Pulley was the first mechanical bird to gain wide acceptance within the Catholic Church. As concepts of socialism began to creep into the world so did the idea that the working man might have something to share with the priestly class. Most notable about this collaboration was the attempt to devise new ways to insult the Muslim and the Jew. And thus the Pulley was invented, much to the delight of the Anglo-Saxons. Problems arose some years later during "Vatican II: The Revenge," which rescinded the use of the Pulley for insulting Semitic people. A small sect of radical Catholics, who actually run the media, still use this anti-Semitic gesture.

INSTRUCTIONS

(1) Extend your bird-giving arm and **(2)** make a fist with your knuckles pointing toward your recipient. **(3)** With your other hand act as though you are grabbing onto a dangling rope that runs through a pulley and is attached to your bird. **(4)** Pull down on the imaginary rope while **(5)** simultaneously extending your bird.

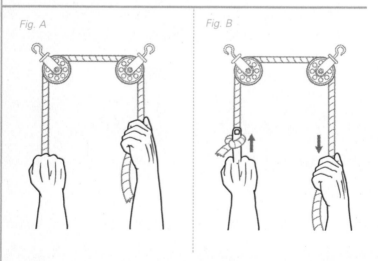

Fig. A

Fig. B

TIP Raise and lower the rope in succession, allowing your finger to extend itself several times in a row, thus giving the recipient a mechanical "booyah."

DIFFICULTY: 🐦🐦🐦 | IMPACT: 🐦🐦🐦🐦 | SPECIALITY: 🐦🐦🐦🐦

THE PUMP

When they hear the word "pump," most twelve-year-old boys might feel slightly uncomfortable. A boy named Travis Bickle had such a reaction one day during a science class demonstration of a vacuum pump. He found himself somewhat aroused by the pumping motion demonstrated by the teacher. His private enjoyment was interrupted when the teacher requested that he come to the front of the class and write the scientific principles of a vacuum on the chalkboard. Desperate and red-faced from the knowledge that his enjoyment would be spotted, he remained in his seat and resorted to subterfuge by pumping up his middle finger and flailing it about. This little act got Travis kicked out of school, but saved him from certain embarrassment. Any twelve-year-old boy would consider this a fair trade.

INSTRUCTIONS

(1) From your elbow, extend your bird-giving arm out in front of you. **(2)** Make a fist with your palm facing up at shoulder level. **(3)** Do the same with your other arm but **(4)** with your palm facing down. **(5)** In a motion perpendicular to the ground, push down with this hand about eight to twelve inches, and then **(6)** return your hand to its original position. Each time you push down on the invisible pump you should **(7)** slowly inflate the bird on your other hand. **(8)** Continue the process until the bird is fully erect.

Fig. A

Fig. B

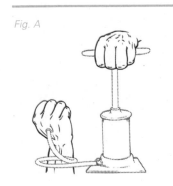
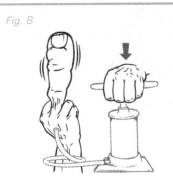

TIP Imagine that you are little Travis Bickle once you have given the recipient the bird, and ask him several times in succession, "You lookin' at me?"

DIFFICULTY: 🐦 🐦 | **IMPACT:** 🐦 🐦 | **SPECIALITY:** 🐦 | 81

CHAPTER TEN

BIRDS OF THE WORLD

No matter where you go in the world you can be sure that someone is going to piss you off. Whether you are in Cairo's Khan al-Khalili, Africa's largest open-air market, or in a French-Canadian pâtisserie in Québec, you can be assured that someone is going to cop an attitude with you.

When traveling abroad, however, the North American bird might not always be your best recourse. So, how do you express that you are tired as hell and that you just aren't going to take it anymore? This section will help you cope with such an eventuality in a manner best befitting each area.

ENGLAND

Leave it to a country with an international reputation as a place where you can actually be killed with kindness to subvert a gesture of peace and love. In the introduction of this book, we speculated on how the Brits might have invented the bird as we know it today. It is our firm belief that now they use *this* gesture to insult people simply because they are a backward people.

INSTRUCTIONS

(1) Make a peace sign. **(2)** Twist your wrist so that your palm and fingers are facing you. **(3)** Throw some bangers and mash at the old boy.

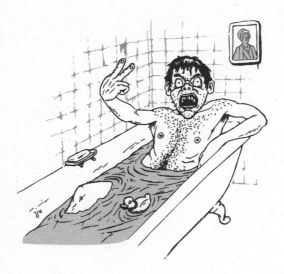

TIP It is important say things like "Jolly good" and "Yes, yes, quite right," or talk about the empire shortly before or after making this gesture. This action should defuse any potential hostility of the average Nigel, but if you are dealing with a soccer yob, take the same precautions you might if you were to run into trouble at a Lynyrd Skynyrd concert.

DIFFICULTY: 🐦 IMPACT: 🐦 🐦 SPECIALTY: 🐦 🐦 🐦

FRANCE

The American version of the bird is widely recognized but not considered appropriately French by the National Academy of Gestures. According to their most recent press release, if you want to "stay French" during this era of unprecedented American gestural imperialism, you should employ this motion when telling someone to get bent.

INSTRUCTIONS

(1) Make two fists. **(2)** Extend one arm toward the recipient with **(3)** a slight bend at the elbow. Take your other hand and **(4)** bring it down in a hacking motion onto the crook of your elbow while **(5)** wrenching your extended arm upward.

TIP We have heard from a Frenchman that if you ever decide use this gesture to express your dissatisfaction with someone from France, you should be prepared for a fight. That is, be prepared for them to launch a verbal assault, but you needn't fear any physical repercussions. No one in France has won a fight since the Middle Ages. Even when two French citizens fight each other, neither can beat the other up.

DIFFICULTY: 🐦🐦   IMPACT: 🐦🐦   SPECIALITY: 🐦🐦

NIGERIA

We found out about this insult when Saddam Hussein asked us to go to Nigeria to secure some weapons-grade uranium for him. We agreed to go on the assignment and signaled so by giving him the thumbs up. He certainly saved us considerable embarrassment when he informed us that the Nigerian people would see this gesture as a statement of aggression. We thanked him for his insight, commended him on his cultural sensitivity, and went on our way, a little bit wiser.

INSTRUCTIONS

(1) Make a fist with **(2)** your palm perpendicular to the ground. **(3)** Raise your thumb.

TIP To make the gesture more offensive, give your arm a little jerk into the air, so as to really say, "Up yours, Nigerian!"

DIFFICULTY: 🐦 | IMPACT: 🐦 🐦 | SPECIALITY: 🐦 🐦 🐦 🐦

GREECE

Greece brought us democracy, philosophy, culture, and lightning. Yes, the Greeks were the height of civilization, but these days they don't do much except work on cashing in on their glorious past. So, if you ever find yourself at the Parthenon surrounded by a gang of souvenir-peddling merchants, you'll find this international bird quite handy. Be prepared for the onslaught of deprecatory epithets that will be hurled upon you, but you can laugh them off since you won't be able to understand them anyway.

INSTRUCTIONS

(1) Place an open-palmed hand between you and your recipient as if you were going to say, "Talk to the hand," **(2)** give the hand a slight push, and **(3)** say, "Na." **(4)** Run!

Na.

TIP According to a Greek American, if you use both hands at the same time and push in the same direction, it is considered an insult of exponential proportions. Also, by closing one eye and placing one hand on your knee, you are not only adding to the insult, but you are also expressing your admiration for Popeye the Sailor Man.

DIFFICULTY: 🐦🐦   IMPACT: 🐦🐦🐦   SPECIALITY: 🐦🐦🐦🐦

SYRIA

It's a hard time to live in North America if you're of Arab descent. That is why we at the *Field Guide to the North American Bird* are pleased to introduce this timeless Syrian insult to a wider American audience. This way, we hope, the next time you are racially profiled at the airport or when buying gas, you can flip off the man behind the counter using the gesture from your heritage, and he will understand the insult. Disseminating important cultural information is what we at the *Guide* are all about.

INSTRUCTIONS

(1) Stick your hand out **(2)** palm facing down with **(3)** your fingers splayed. Then **(4)** point your bird toward the ground and **(5)** wiggle it.

 TIP If you happen to be a cop, please forget you read the above paragraph.

DIFFICULTY: 🐦🐦 IMPACT: 🐦 SPECIALITY: 🐦🐦🐦🐦

CHAPTER ELEVEN

REJECTED BIRDS

When you begin giving others the bird using this handbook, you will definitely notice their excitement at seeing new variations on an old gesture. They will attempt to match your clever reinterpretation with one of their own. In some cases they will be funny, but most of the time they will be just stupid.

In doing research for this book a great number of people were flipped off, and many of them, if not most, had suggestions of their own. This section includes a few of the birds that just didn't cut the mustard or that we thought had potential but never quite made it off the drawing board. Basically, these are the birds that we gave the finger.

THE KANGAROO

When our oldest brother, Jared, invented this bird in an attempt to ingratiate himself into the family project, it became all too evident that his skills were not quite up to snuff. After sitting around with him in his apartment while he barraged us with one horrible bird after another, he came up with this sorry excuse for a bird, which is just lame enough to make the reject list.

INSTRUCTIONS

(1) Take your nesting bird and spin it around so that it is pointing at the ground. **(2)** Make a bird with your other hand and face it in the same direction. **(3)** Place the tip of one bird onto the knuckle of the other as if it were resting in a pouch. **(4)** Hop them around together.

TIP This bird works worst when you actually find a surface where you can make the Kangaroo jump around as if it were somewhere in the Outback. Then begin laughing uncontrollably at your own cunning wit. At least that is how it was presented to us.

DIFFICULTY: 🦃🦃🦃 IMPACT: 🦃 SPECIALITY: 🦃🦃🦃

THE WINDSHIELD WIPERS

This one was created by an up-and-coming young comedy writer who was determined to construct a new and innovative bird, with one catch: he was actually aiming for one that would be considered a reject. He did a great job, as we could not find one potential application for this bird.

INSTRUCTIONS

(1) Start by giving the Double (page 12). **(2)** Rotate your wrists in a side-to-side motion as if they were windshield wipers.

TIP The creator of the Windshield Wipers was fond of spouting the most vulgar expletives he could think of while executing this bird. You should follow his example. A little saliva collecting in the corner of your mouth doesn't hurt either.

THE HEISMAN

Our attempt to make a series of posing birds is based upon a joke that we used to use when we were kids. One of us would ask our mother if we could pose a question. When she said, "Sure," we would contort ourselves into the best weight-lifting pose we could pull off and ask, "What's for dinner?" We tried using this same principle by inserting a bird into American icons like Mount Rushmore, the Statue of Liberty, or the Heisman Trophy. But, as the running joke of our childhood goes, every idea we came up with was just stupid.

INSTRUCTIONS

(1) Lean forward while you **(2)** balance yourself on a slightly bent leg and **(3)** bring your other knee up near your chest as if you were running. **(4)** Bend your other arm at the elbow and **(5)** cup your hand as if you were carrying a ball. **(6)** Stick your bird-giving arm straight out in front of you and **(7)** flip the bird.

TIP Next time you are at a student protest, strike a pose as the Statue of Liberty, but instead of holding a torch, display your bird proudly. We'd love to hear what kind of reaction you get from the campus police or National Guard.

DIFFICULTY: 🐾🐾🐾🐾 IMPACT: 🐾 SPECIALITY: 🐾🐾🐾🐾

THE SALOON

When we needed to figure out new ways to flip each other off, it was natural to branch out into genre films for inspiration. We didn't concern ourselves with the impact that the birds might have on strangers, which, in the case of the Saloon, is about none. We always had to explain that it meant, "You are walking into the land of Fuck You, you know, through saloon doors from the old West. . . ." Even after the explanation this bird had little impact. Still it is one we gain much joy out of doing to one another.

INSTRUCTIONS

(1) Start by giving the Double (page 12). **(2)** Rotate your wrists so that the tips of the birds are just about touching, parallel to the ground. **(3)** With a slight movement from your wrist, swing a bird toward your body and **(4)** make a small creaky sound. Then, act as though that movement mirrors the opening of a door that swings in both directions, and **(5)** let your bird swing back in the opposite direction slightly less far than it did in the previous direction. **(6)** Continue this process until the bird is stationary in its original position.

TIP Don't perform this bird unless you are prepared to explain yourself later or unless you are like crazy Uncle Morty who always tells bad jokes and then elbows you and says, "Get it, get it?" after he explains it to you.

DIFFICULTY: | IMPACT: | SPECIALITY: | 95

THE TALL MAN

When we finally rejected this idea the entire office hung their heads down in shame. The original clean-cut children's version of this song was an inspiration to all of us to learn the names of the fingers of the hand and is a nostalgic favorite. It became obvious, though, that this bird was just too cumbersome an operation to be effective. We play-acted several potential performances, but there was just no getting around the fact that to start with thumbkin and sing the whole song made the gesture fall flat. By the time you get to the bird, your recipient will have had two extra slices of pizza and your portion of the cola.

INSTRUCTIONS

(1) Place both arms behind your back. **(2)** Sing, "Where is tall man?" while **(3)** you bring one arm out in front of you, palm facing the receiver **(4)** with your bird fully extended. **(5)** Repeat steps 2 through 4 with your other arm. With both birds now flying **(6)** say, "Here I am!" **(7)** as you have one bird take a bow. **(8)** Repeat steps 6 and 7 with the other bird. **(9)** Say, "Run and hide," as **(10)** you place one arm back behind you. **(11)** Repeat step 9 as you place your other arm behind you.

Fig. A

Fig. B

TIP Give this bird a shot with a group of kids who are trying to learn the song. Even if they do get it, they'll probably just start crying, you evil son of a bitch.

DIFFICULTY: 🦅🦅🦅🦅 | IMPACT: 🦅 | SPECIALITY: 🦅🦅🦅🦅

ABOUT THE AUTHORS

ADAM BLANK grew up in Des Moines, Iowa, before attending Hampshire College in western Massachusetts. After college, he moved to Portland, Oregon, where he worked with adolescents in the social service system. A career shift placed him in the film industry, where he worked as a production assistant in documentaries, infomercials, commercials, and feature films. Having had his fill of out-of-control teens and advertising company bigwigs, he moved back to the East Coast and created his own film company, Jigsaw Films.

Adam's work in both the social services and the film industry have prepared him for his crowning achievement: this book. His time in the psychological trenches helped him understand the mindset of the average birder, and working with advertising executives thickened his skin enough that he can now withstand a constant onslaught of birding, unfazed and unimpressed.

LAUREN BLANK also grew up in Des Moines, Iowa, and received her B.A. in East Asian Studies at Lewis and Clark College in Portland, Oregon. After college, she became a guide for Where There Be Dragons, an organization that leads American teens on cross-country backpacking trips in China. She has also worked for the Portland Classical Chinese Garden and taught English in Taiwan.

She currently resides in Jackson Hole, Wyoming, and is one third of an elite crime-fighting rock-climbing team known as the Climbing Devils. Lauren's fluency in Mandarin Chinese as well as her ability to reach great heights as a climber have allowed her birding skills to soar well above those of the average birder.

MICHAEL H. MOORE was born in Iowa of good stock in the year 1970. At a young age, he was schooled in music and art by his inspired and broadminded kin. As a young man, he forged strength and tenacity through hard labor—and harder drinking—in farm fields and factories across Polk County. After witnessing a few grisly industrial accidents and drinking deep from the cup of moral depravity brewed daily in suburban Iowa, Michael decided it best to flee the bosom of his family and beloved state.

He moved to the New York City to learn the black arts of graphic design and atonal musical composition. One day he met an old friend from his schooling days, Adam Blank, who nearly ran him into the street out of shock at being spotted by a fellow countryman. Epithets were exchanged followed by obscene gestures and near glancing blows when Adam's attention was commanded by the lightning fast flash of Michael's grotesque and knobby middle fingers.

So struck was Adam by the size and agility of those digits, that he stopped in his tracks. He realized that Michael could be useful, despite his shoddy hygiene and ciphering skills. Right there on the street, a deal was struck and sealed with spit in such a fashion that the bystanders who had gathered around the boisterous pair thought it prudent to take their distance. This book is the result of the deal made on that fateful day.

What Bird Did That?
A Driver's Guide to Some Common Birds of North America
by Peter Hansard and Burton Silver

The first scholarly treatment of ornithological dejecta, commonly known as bird droppings. With full-color illustrations of splattered bird droppings, this handy glove-compartment guide enables you to quickly identify which species was responsible for the display on your windshield. The excreta of a wide variety of avian species are fully described, with detailed notes on the animal's food, geographic location, and the best methods of starting a collection. An invaluable companion for those who wish to learn more about birds and what they do.

5 x 8½ inches, 64 pages, ISBN 0-89815-427-8

Who Cut the Cheese?
A Cultural History of the Fart
by Jim Dawson

What exactly is a fart? Why do we do it? Why do we hide it when we do it? And why do we find farts so darn funny? Author Jim Dawson sniffs out a load of historical and scientific fart tales, then offers the kind of fun facts you'll be dying to let slip at social occasions, in chapters like "Fart Facts That Aren't Just Hot Air," "Gone with the Wind" (on famous movie farts), and "Le Petomane & the Art of the Fart" (on the most famous windbag in history). From fact to fiction to frivolous flatulence, this book is unquestionably a ripping good read.

6 x 9 inches, 192 pages, ISBN 1-58008-011-1